The Best Man's Wedding

from confetti.co.uk
don't get married without us…

First published in 2003 by Octopus Publishing Group,
2–4 Heron Quays, London, E14 4JP
www.conran-octopus.co.uk

A catalogue record for this book is available
from the British Library.

ISBN 1 84091 305 3

Publishing Director Lorraine Dickey
Senior Editor Katey Day
Assistant Editor Sybella Marlow
Creative Director Leslie Harrington
Designer Victoria Burley
Senior Production Controller Manjit Sihra

Contents

Introduction 4

Duties before the wedding day 8

The stag night 40

Wedding day duties 66

The speech 94

Final words of wisdom 126

THE BEST MAN'S WEDDING

Well, it's finally happened – you've been asked to be a best man! So, what does being a best man involve?

What are your responsibilities?

What about the speech?

This book will answer these and all your other questions.

INTRODUCTION

Historically, a bridegroom chose the best man for his strength and fighting skills, to assist him when he captured his bride.

A best man's support was also needed on the wedding day to protect the bride from any rival who might try to carry her off.

THE BEST MAN'S WEDDING

Today the best man has become exclusively the groom's escort while the bride is supported by her bridesmaids.

The role of best man (or best woman) is offered to the groom's closest adult relative or friend and is not one that should be accepted lightly.

INTRODUCTION

You will be a main player not only on the wedding day, but your advice and practical help will be much needed in the preparations beforehand.

For some reassurance, or if you just want to ask a question about the role, get on to the For Him message board on confetti's website – check out www.confetti.co.uk/cafe/default.asp

Duties before the wedding day

The run-up to the big day

As you'll soon discover, the best man's job
starts well before the stag night…

Your tasks are many and varied but
essentially, during the run-up to the
wedding, you will be relied upon as a
supporter and organizer.

**Here are some acceptable reasons
for refusing the role:**
- A prior engagement on the day
- A previous liaison with the bride
- Illness or disability
- You don't know the groom that well and
  are not sure why you've been asked
  (but don't give this as a reason!)

If in doubt, refuse in time for someone else
to be asked and before money has been spent.

These are unacceptable reasons for refusing the role:
- You don't have any respect for the bride
- You just don't want to have to organize the stag night
- You get a better offer for that day later on
- You can't afford it

Once you've accepted, it's important that the groom feels he can rely on you for ongoing support, especially on the day.

Call a family huddle

It can be a good idea to arrange to meet with the groom, the bride and her parents and chat about how you can help with the wedding arrangements. If you don't already know each other, it's also a chance to meet before the big day.

Call a family huddle

Everyone will get an opportunity to voice their opinions, and this is the time to allocate jobs and duties. Explain the purpose of the get-together beforehand so people can arrive prepared with any thoughts they may have.

Scout locations

If possible, visit the bride and groom's chosen ceremony and reception venues. By familiarizing yourself with the layouts you'll feel much more prepared on the day.

Scout locations

To ensure the smooth running of play on the day, it might be wise to note things like timings between venues, locations of entrances and exits, car-parking facilities and access, particularly if there will be disabled guests.

Getting the boys in

The groom and best man traditionally get together to choose the ushers, although the groom might want to do this by himself. As best man, you need to make sure the ushers are aware of their responsibilities, recognize the key family members and are generally charming and helpful on the day.

Getting the boys in

They should also be aware – thanks to you – of any special seating requirements, such as guests in wheelchairs, who may need extra space and perhaps help getting to their places. Ushers should also make sure that the seats at the front of the ceremony venue reserved for close family members are not taken by other guests.

On the move

You may have to arrange the transport for the wedding day. Ask the bride's parents how many cars to order and if they'd like you to get quotes and make the booking.

An average order would be two cars from the bride's home to the ceremony venue and three from there to the reception – the third car being for the newlyweds.

DUTIES BEFORE THE WEDDING DAY

On the move

Crucially, it's your job to get the groom to the venue on time and in one piece, for which you may prefer to rely on your own transport. It's good to have the number of a local taxi firm in case you or any guests run into any problems. Also, carry maps to the venues and if you don't have a mobile phone, borrow one. Just make sure it's switched off during the ceremony.

How to look sharp

Together with the groom, decide on the outfits for both yourselves and the ushers. It's usual for each person to pay for his own hire cost.

If hiring morning dress, try to get everyone together for the fittings or at least ensure they all go to the same supplier. At the very least, phone round and make sure that all the men know what they're supposed to be wearing and from which shop.

How to look sharp

If the bridegroom is unable to collect the outfits then this duty will also fall to you. Be sure to check that the outfits are complete. Don't forget to find out where the buttonholes for you and the groom will be on the wedding day – you'll need them before other guests do.

Check out confetti's menswear database plus tips on buying and hire at www.confetti.co.uk/men/default.asp

How to tie ties

Here you'll find simple instructions for the four classic tie styles.

The Bow Tie

1

2

3

4

5

6

DUTIES BEFORE THE WEDDING DAY

The Bow Tie
The bow tie should be tied as follows:

1. Start with A one and a half inches below B
2. Take A over then under B
3. Double B in half and place across the collar points
4. Hold B with thumb and index finger; drop A over
5. Pull A through a little, then double A and pass behind, then through the hole in front
6. Poke resulting loop through; even it out, then tighten

The Four in Hand

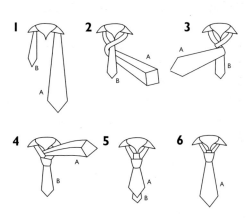

The Four in Hand

The Four in Hand should be tied as follows:

1. Start with A about 20 inches below B
2. Take A behind B
3. Continue wrapping right round
4. Pull A up through the loop
5. Pull A down through loop in front
6. Tighten

And that's it!

The Windsor

1

2

3

4

5

6

The Windsor

The Windsor should be tied as follows:

1. Start with A about 24 inches below B
2. Take A behind B and up through loop
3. Bring A over and behind B
4. Take A down through loop again
5. Then over and up through loop
6. Bring through the knot and tighten

And that's it!

The Half Windsor

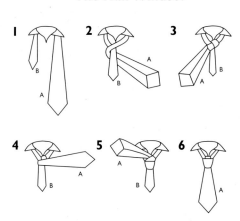

The Half Windsor

A Half Windsor is a kind of reverse Windsor.

1. Start in the same position as the Windsor
2. Loop A behind B
3. Bring A up into the loop and out behind B on the other side
4. Fold A back across B
5. Tuck A up through the loop
6. Bring A back through the knot and tighten

The big speech
Yours tends to be the last of the speeches on the big day, following the father of the bride and the groom.

On the plus side, guests will generally be 'warmed up' and ready to laugh; on the more daunting side, their expectations may be higher.

For more suggestions, see page 94.

The big speech

Would we leave you to do this on your own? Of course not! For ideas meet us at www.confetti.co.uk/men/default.asp

Stag night

It's your responsibility to organize the stag
night, the groom's traditional farewell
to single life.

You may want the groom to be the butt of
a few jokes, but the point of a stag night
should be an opportunity for affectionate
celebration, rather than pre-planned pranks.

For more suggestions, see page 40.

Stag night

Pssst! We know this great stag night location… loads in fact… www.confetti.co.uk/confetti_pages /default.asp

Dress rehearsal

You'll definitely need to turn up to any wedding run-through that's been planned. This will give you a chance to familiarize yourself with the layout of the venue and get a better grasp of your role in the proceedings. Just knowing exactly where to stand and what to do on the big day will help soothe your nerves.

Dress rehearsal

The rehearsal may also be a good chance for you to make sure that the fees are paid in advance to those involved in the ceremony: officiant or registrar, organist, bell-ringers, singers, musicians.

Pre-wedding checklist

Here are some useful tips plus your traditional responsibilities during the run-up to the wedding day:

• Be involved in discussions and decisions in the planning stage with the groom, acting as a sounding board for his ideas

Pre-wedding checklist

• Help the groom choose the ushers, who are usually picked from both the bride and groom's families and friends

• Make sure the ushers are aware of their responsibilities, that they attend fittings of outfits and are available to attend the rehearsal (if required)

Pre-wedding checklist

- Together with the groom, decide on the outfits for both yourselves, and the ushers. If the outfits are hired, it is usual to expect each to pay for his own hire, unless the groom says otherwise

- Prepare your speech well in advance (see page 94 for more advice and ideas)

- Attend the wedding rehearsal and check car-parking facilities and access, particularly if there will be disabled guests

Pre-wedding checklist

• Arrange the stag night for at least a few
days before the wedding to give everyone
a chance to recover

(see page 40 for more advice and ideas)

• Collect any hire outfits if the bridegroom
is unable to and check that the outfits
are complete

• Find out where you can collect
buttonholes for yourself and the groom
on the wedding day

The stag night

THE STAG NIGHT

Forget all that 'last days of freedom' stuff.
Today's stag dos are all about originality
and style! For a truly unforgettable
pre-wedding bash, start planning early
and get creative.

Don't forget the toys! We're talking toy
guns, table torpedoes and bazookas that
spray confetti everywhere – you'll be
noticed! Check out
www.confetti.co.uk/shopping/default.asp

The most important thing to do is to work out how many people you want to invite and compile a guest list with the groom.

Get all the contact details of who he wants to invite from him and try to get in touch with everyone as soon as possible, to maximize the chances of everyone being free at the same time.

THE STAG NIGHT

Remember, this is your opportunity to really take charge and concoct a memorable event for the groom and the other guys in the party, so don't leave things to chance. You can make the difference between just another night in the pub and a legendary send-off – and no, it's not down to your karaoke performance of 'My Way'.

It's a date

Despite tradition, it's not now considered a good idea to plan the stag party the night before the big day. Ideally, hold it a week before the wedding or, even better, during the same weekend as the bride's hen night. This means the couple have as many free weekends together as possible to plan the the wedding and won't lose out on any precious time together.

Paying up

Cash-wise, everyone generally pays for themselves and chips in to cover the groom too. It's less hassle to ask everyone to contribute towards a kitty before you go out. If you're spending a weekend away, send everyone a note or e-mail asking them for a cheque in advance to cover their costs. Make it clear that unless they pay up you can't reserve their place.

Top ideas

Do you want to spend a weekend being active? Being creative or cultural? In the lap of luxury? Or do you want a traditional boozy weekend?

Top ideas

Do you want to party close to home, or would a weekend away go down well? Maybe you want to go abroad for a stag weekend to really remember.

Whatever you decide, here are some great ideas for group activities.

For clubbers

If you want to rave the night away, bear in mind that many clubs have a strict door policy, so phone your chosen club in advance to check you're welcome – and ask if they offer group discounts.

Alternatively, book a party bus tour of London nightclubs: wine and beer on the bus, plus all entry fees are usually included in the price.

For daredevils

Adrenaline junkies could book up for a stag bungee jump, or take to the skies in a stunt plane to loop the loop and barrel roll! White-water rafting, trapezing above lakes and rivers on a zip wire or zooming about in a powerboat off the coast are great ideas for summer stags.

For action men

Organize a day of paintballing where you can team up and practise your SAS skills, or how about dry-slope skiing or snowboarding for a day's action.

Or, if the budget's tight, organize a game of football or rounders in a local park and follow it up by after-action pints in a favourite pub.

THE STAG NIGHT

For boy racers

Take to the roads on an exhilarating driving stag: choose from a day at Brands Hatch pushing a Ferrari to its limits; tearing across rough terrain in a 4x4 or competing against your mates in a go-karting race.

THE BEST MAN'S WEDDING

For party animals

Pack your bags for a mad weekend of partying! The most popular places to head for include Amsterdam, Barcelona and Dublin.

Get quotes from travel agents to give everyone a costing before they commit themselves. Once you've got a firm number, ask everyone for full payment before booking.

THE STAG NIGHT

For modern couples

Take inspiration from Sophie and Edward, who opted for a joint hen and stag – they invited ten friends each for a weekend at a country house, to horse-ride and play ball!

If you're not related to anyone on the civil list however, you and the chief bridesmaid could cook a meal at your home or hers and invite the happy couple and guests for dinner and silly board games.

For gamblers

Organize a night at the dogs or set up a
mini casino at home. Specialist companies
supply gaming tables, accessories, croupiers
and funny money for an authentic touch!
For an ultimate weekend of gambling, fly
out to Las Vegas on Friday afternoon.
This is a 24-hour city with no 'last orders'!

Carry on camping

Borrow a couple of tents, jump into a
camper van and head off to the seaside or
the dales. Remember to take sausages,
marshmallows and a guitar.
Oh – and a torch.

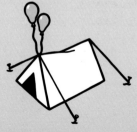

For drinkers

Spice up a basic pub crawl by adding dares,
getting your mates to each tell a relevant
story about the groom in a different pub
or playing pub golf.
Or you could even make one of your
stops a karaoke bar...

THE STAG NIGHT

For drinkers

Why not get together in a gang and set off to Blackpool for a weekend's home-grown seaside fun? Trawl along the promenade for slot machines and cheap boozers, before making yourself sick on The Big One, the world's highest rollercoaster.

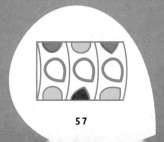

On course

Pick a top golf course like Valderrama, Gleneagles or La Manga, and organize your own Masters Championship. No need to carry your clubs here, just make sure you've got plenty of drinks stashed away in the buggy.

Chill out

Who says that stag weekends have to be
about getting plastered? Why not go to a
spa retreat or health farm? Book you and
your mates in for massage therapy, to
cleanse your mind and body so you'll be
completely relaxed come the big day.

Horsey horsey

Don't just stop at a day at the races, go for the double! Combine Chester and Aintree, Lingfield and Epsom, or Doncaster and York to give yourself twice as many opportunities of winning enough cash to cover all those last-minute wedding expenses.

A wee dram (or two)

Take the train to Inverness, the middle of
the Scottish Highlands, and home of the
whisky distillery. Having canvassed opinion
among your group to the most-favoured
single malt, arrange a distillery tour and
stay over after a meal of traditional
Scottish fayre.

On the piste

For a more extravagant send-off, why settle for the dry ski-slope when a weekend skiing in France or Switzerland is a short flight away? Take an early morning flight and you can be sipping gluhwein on the slopes by midday. Just don't let the groom break a leg – it won't look good on the wedding pics.

On the piste

So, put on your thinking cap and
get planning!
www.confetti.co.uk/confetti_pages
/default.asp

On the day or night

It's your responsibility to look after the groom and make sure he will return in one piece. The bride will know who to blame if he doesn't! Don't let the groom attempt to do anything or drink any more than he could normally cope with.

Don't let people play tricks on him that may not seem funny in the morning – such as dyeing his hair blue or sending him off on a cross-channel ferry!

On the day or night

It's important to keep the pace of the evening steady. If a lot of alcohol is involved, don't let everyone – especially not the groom! – get too drunk too soon.

For heaven's sake make sure the crimes of the memorable event are recorded on film!

Disposable cameras available at
www.confetti.co.uk/shopping/default.asp

Wedding day duties

The wedding day

A best man's role on the wedding day is of the utmost importance.

The groom will no doubt be very nervous and calm support is vital.

The following pages explain in detail just what you need to do to ensure everything runs smoothly on the day…

Morning checklist

- Meet the groom at least a couple of hours before you need to leave for the ceremony venue and help ensure he looks his best

- Check the groom has everything he will need for the honeymoon especially the tickets and passports. Make sure you put the honeymoon luggage in the right vehicle

WEDDING DAY DUTIES

Morning checklist

- Collect the buttonholes for the groom, ushers and yourself

- It's traditional to check with the bride about final arrangements and any last-minute messages you might need

Before setting off

Most importantly, make sure you have the ring(s) and money for the church fees (civil wedding fees will have been paid beforehand). A telephone call to the bride's father telling him when you are leaving will be welcome! Take the groom to the ceremony venue, making sure you arrive at least 30 minutes before the ceremony is due to begin. Check you have some confetti, if the venue allows it. Choose from 70 different kinds on www.confetti.co.uk/shopping/default.asp

At the ceremony venue

Make sure you have the rings (again).
Check the order of service sheets have
been brought to the venue to hand
to guests as they arrive.

At the ceremony venue

Make sure your ushers are wearing their buttonholes. If buttonholes have been ordered for guests, check they have been delivered to the venue.

Get the ushers in line! Organize one on each side of the entrance to hand out order of service sheets. If the couple are following a traditional seating plan, make sure the ushers know to direct the bride's relatives to the left-hand side of the church and the groom's relatives to the right.

At the ceremony venue

If the bride and groom have a page boy
or ring bearer in the wedding party, have
a chat, man to man. Make sure he knows
when he'll need to step up to the
mark with the rings.

If the ceremony is in a church, you will need to:

• Pay the church fees on behalf of the groom and check one last time you've got those rings.

• Take your seat with the groom on the front right-hand pew while waiting for the bride. Shortly before the bride arrives, you will be prompted to stand in position at the head of the aisle, to the groom's right.

WEDDING DAY DUTIES

If the ceremony is in a church, you will need to:

• Hand over the ring(s) at the right time during the ceremony – your big moment.

• After the service, accompany the chief bridesmaid (or matron of honour) and the bride and groom to the vestry for the signing of the register.
You may also be asked by the groom to sign the register as a witness.

If the ceremony is in a church, you will need to:

• Join the recessional down the aisle following in line after the bride and groom, the bride's father and groom's mother and the groom's father and the bride's mother. Escort the chief bridesmaid from the church on your left arm.

If the ceremony is at a register office or a licensed venue, you will need to:

• Take your seat with the groom on the front right-hand seats while waiting for the bride to arrive. Shortly before the bride enters, you will be prompted to stand in position before the registrar, to the groom's right.

If the ceremony is at a register office or a licensed venue, you will need to:

• Hand over the ring(s) at the required moment as prompted by the registrar.

• Sign the register as a witness, if asked to by the groom.

If the ceremony is at a register office or a licensed venue, you will need to:

• Join the recessional out of the room, following in line after the bride and groom, the bride's father with the groom's mother and the groom's father with the bride's mother. Escort the chief bridesmaid on your left arm.

Immediately after the ceremony, your duties are to:

- Help the photographer in grouping guests together for photographs if necessary.

WEDDING DAY DUTIES

Immediately after the ceremony, your duties are to:

• Make sure that all the guests have directions and transport to the reception, arranging lifts where needed.

• Make sure that you leave for the reception venue with the bridesmaids immediately after the bride and groom so that you arrive shortly after.

Let's celebrate !

When you get to the reception venue, your duties are as follows, though some will depend on whether you have agreed to take on the role of toastmaster:

Collect any messages from the bride's father and check to see if any messages have been delivered directly to the reception venue

Let's celebrate !

Join the receiving line, if asked to by the
hosts, to greet and welcome guests as they
move into the reception room and help
them find their places

When everyone is seated and before the
meal or buffet is served, call for silence and
introduce the couple to the reception
room as newlyweds

Let's celebrate !

When the meal is finished, call for silence and introduce the speeches. Invite the bride's father to speak first.

After the bride's father has delivered his speech and toasted the bride and groom, introduce the groom for his much awaited words!

Let's celebrate !

The groom's speech ends with a toast to
the bridesmaids. You will reply to this toast
on behalf of the bridesmaids and deliver
your speech, read congratulations from
absent family and friends, and close by
toasting the bride and groom.

Once the speeches have concluded, you
can breathe a sigh of relief and announce
the cutting of the cake.

Party time !

Now the big speech is out of the way
you can relax a little.

It's tradition to dance with the chief
bridesmaid first, joining the bride and
groom mid-way through the first dance.

WEDDING DAY DUTIES

Party time !

Your responsibilities are not over yet,
however. You need to keep a general eye
on the proceedings to ensure that
everything is running smoothly. If wedding
cameras have been put out on the guests'
tables, for example, ensure they are used
throughout the reception.

Party time !

Have fun supervising the decoration of the groom's car — or whatever transport is taking them away from the venue that evening. But make sure that whatever you do is this side of criminal damage or that you've consulted a good lawyer.

Party time !

The happy – and hapless – couple will be
relying on it, so bear in mind that the
car needs to remain in working order,
especially if they are going straight off on
their honeymoon and need to catch trains
or flights later.

Party time !

Finally, assist the hosts in bringing the celebrations to a close, making sure everyone has transport home or can find their room if they are staying overnight at the reception venue.

Party time !

The hosts – especially if they are the bride
and groom – may appreciate it if you offer
to check the bill and ensure any
outstanding payments are settled at
the end of the night.

Party time !

When you leave the venue, take a last look round for any stray presents or lost property. Collect them together and keep them safe until you can return them to their rightful owners.

Party time !

As soon as possible after the wedding, arrange to collect any hired outfits so that they can be returned and deposits refunded. Make sure any items left at the venue find their way back to their owners.

The speech

THE SPEECH

Does the thought of preparing a speech for your best mate's entire family and friends bring you out in a cold sweat?

Fear not! Here is all the help you will need for your big moment...

See the confetti books *How to Write a Wedding Speech* and *Wedding Speeches*, also in this series, for more advice and ideas.

The speech

Of all the speeches at the wedding reception, the guests generally look forward to the best man's speech the most.

Start preparing your speech several weeks before the day. Bear in mind that the aim of your speech is to give some background to the groom for the benefit of the bride's side of the family.

The speech

Essentially, the more prepared you are, and the more confident you are about giving your speech, the more your audience will enjoy it – and so will you.

However, at this late stage in the proceedings, they probably don't want quite the same privileged insight into the groom as you have.

Research is the key

If you're stuck for stories or ideas, get
together with friends and relatives
for reminiscences.

Plan a casual evening together so people
aren't aware of your research gathering,
and get them to tell their funny and
favourite stories about the groom.

Research is the key

While they sit there swapping stories, you may find the bulk of your speech will have been written for you by the end of the night.

Other sources

Look through your old photo albums,
letters and cuttings, or even note books
from your school or university days – any
of these might provide something funny
to read out or hold up.

Other sources

Track down people the groom went to school or worked with, former teachers and even bosses, to see what they remember about the groom. You never know who may have an amusing story to tell.

Look to the stars

Another possible source of good material
is horoscopes. Find out the star signs of
your subjects, look into the typical
associated characteristics and traits, and
compare them with the people you're
talking about.

Look to the stars

Much fun can be had, especially where the typical qualities don't match… or where the star sign's vices do! Other ways to use horoscopes include finding books that discuss star-sign compatibility. For ideas see *Compatibility,* also in this series.

Scour the archives

Track down a newspaper for the day your
subject was born and try to find an article
that will fit the person you are writing
about, or adapt a story to suit.

Scour the archives

You might be able to get an old photograph and incorporate it into the article. Try to make it look authentic and then get the whole thing blown up as big as possible to display while you're speaking. With a little imagination this could be very amusing.

What's in a name?

More material can be found by looking at
the couple's names, and researching what
they really mean. Most names are associated
with specific qualities which you can pick up
on and compare with the person.

What's in a name?

If you're trying to make a sincere point about someone's qualities, the fact that their name comes from the Latin for 'strength' or 'love', for example, can be a striking way of underlining the message.

Make 'em laugh

As for finding jokes, the field is enormous. Rent out comedy videos and films, look up gags on the net, and note down funnies in papers and magazines. There are plenty of wedding joke books around, too.

THE SPEECH

Make 'em laugh

You could source material by asking people
for their favourite joke.
But remember, very often your own raw
original material and amusing stories will
be much funnier than any stuff that
you've borrowed.

Make sure you establish a link with
the wedding to ensure it goes
down well.

Suitable material

Only use safe, gentle humour, relevant for the situation and appropriate for ALL the wedding guests – including children, older people and maiden aunts.

Suitable material

Emotions run high at weddings, so avoid
material that could unwittingly cause
offence. Avoid anything gross, smutty or
disturbing, as well as mean-spirited gags
at the expense of mothers-in-law,
women drivers, etc.

Suitable material

Criticizing anyone present – especially the bride who, don't forget, is the star of the show – or making jokes at people's expense can also alienate guests.

Similarly, criticizing anything about the wedding itself, such as the venue or service is not a good idea.

THE SPEECH

Suitable material

As a rule, if you can rehearse your speech
in front of your mum and your granny so
that they don't feel uncomfortable and
without you feeling embarrassed, then
you're on to a winner!

Delivering your speech

Proper preparation will really pay off on the day – ad-libbing will lead only to hesitation and rambling.

It is important that everyone can hear you, so if you have not spoken to an audience before, practise projecting your voice.

THE SPEECH

Delivering your speech

A good joke can be ruined by poor delivery. No one will laugh at something they can't hear properly, so speak clearly and slowly and don't gabble.

Delivering your speech

If the joke fails and nobody laughs, then
make the failure the joke. Comics often
use staple rescue lines such as
'Only me on that one then' or, glancing
round at an imaginary assistant,
'Start the car!'

Using prompts

Write the speech out beforehand and take time to get it right. Practice really does make perfect! Use brief notes that remind you of each bit of the speech, written in order, in very neat writing. If you use a word processor, choose a large font.

Using prompts

Gradually cut back your text, so the notes say just as much as you need to remind you of what you want to say. This will be infinitely more impressive than reading a whole speech hidden behind a quivering sheet of paper.

THE SPEECH

Stage fright

Don't panic! If you're really suffering from nerves, let your audience know.
Begin with something like 'The following speech is brought to you in association with Imodium.'

Try not to drink too much before your speech, even if it is tempting to have a bit of Dutch courage!

Stage fright

Most importantly, bear in mind that everyone is on your side. Remember to breathe, stand still and make the speech at normal conversational pace.

Eye contact is vital – you'll be surprised how much it helps you to relax and connect with your audience.

Stage fright

Speak slowly and try not to race through your speech – people may not hear you properly or may not have time to take in what you say, which could result in your jokes dying a death.

.

Speech checklist

Here are some handy checkpoints of what to include in your big speech:

• After the groom finishes his speech (traditionally ending by thanking the bridesmaids), it is usual for the best man to begin by thanking the groom for his toast to the bridesmaids and to praise the team of bridesmaids, pageboys and ushers

Speech checklist

- Read any telegrams and messages from guests unable to attend the wedding

- Remember to address the couple, and especially talk to and about the bride. Too many best man's speeches almost entirely overlook her

Speech checklist

• To the main task – embarrassing the groom! Entertain the guests by giving them an amusing insight into the groom's more unfortunate misdeeds, bearing in mind these must be suitable for granny to listen to as well as your peers

Speech checklist

- If you need to, give any information about the reception to the guests after your main speech

- Conclude with a toast to the bride and groom

- If the bride is making a speech, you will need to introduce her after your speech

Final words of wisdom

Don't worry about your role or responsibilities and don't let the pressure get to you – after all, the groom has chosen you because he thinks you're the best man for the job!

Final words of wisdom

If you're well prepared and stay calm you'll be able to handle any little crisis that occurs before the wedding or on the big day itself, as well as laying on a stag night to end all stag nights.

Despite the preparation and planning for the most important day of your best friend's life, remember – above all, enjoy it!

ABOUT CONFETTI.CO.UK

Confetti.co.uk is the UK's leading weddings and special occasion website, helping more than 300,000 brides, grooms and guests every month.

To find out more or to order your confetti gift book, party brochure or wedding stationery brochure, visit www.confetti.co.uk email info@confetti.co.uk

visit Confetti, 80 Tottenham Court Road, London W1 or call 0870 840 6060

Some of the other books in this comprehensive series: *The Bridesmaid's Wedding*, *Your Daughter's Wedding*, *Men At Weddings*, and *Wedding Planner*